# EARTHWORMS

## TEACHER'S GUIDE

Grades 6–10

### Skills
Observing, Measuring, Experimenting,
Predicting, Averaging, Graphing, Interpreting Data, Inferring

### Concepts
Pulse Rates, Cold-Blooded Animals, Effects of Temperature,
Circulatory System, Adaptation

### Themes
Systems & Interactions, Stability, Patterns of Change,
Evolution, Structure, Energy, Diversity & Unity

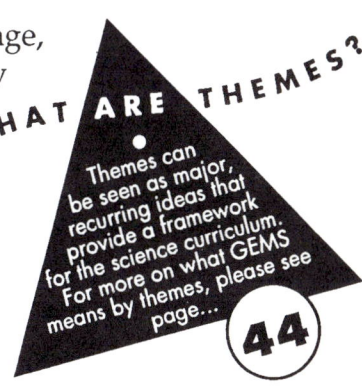

WHAT ARE THEMES?
Themes can be seen as major, recurring ideas that provide a framework for the science curriculum. For more on what GEMS means by themes, please see page... 44

### Nature of Science and Mathematics
Scientific Community, Interdisciplinary,
Cooperative Efforts, Creativity & Constraints,
Theory-Based and Testable,
Changing Nature of Facts and Theories,
Objectivity & Ethics,
Real-Life Applications

### Time
Three 45-minute sessions

Robert C. Knott
Kimi Hosoume
Lincoln Bergman

LHS GEMS

LIBRARY
Antioch New England Graduate School
40 Avon St
Keene NH 03431-3516

**Great Explorations in Math and Science (GEMS)**
Lawrence Hall of Science
University of California at Berkeley

**Illustrations**
Rose Craig
Lisa Klofkorn
Carol Bevilacqua

**Photographs**
Richard Hoyt

Lawrence Hall of Science, University of California, Berkeley, CA 94720. Chairman: Glenn T. Seaborg; Director: Marian C. Diamond

Publication was made possible by grants from the A.W. Mellon Foundation and the Carnegie Corporation of New York. This support does not imply responsibility for statements or views expressed in publications of the GEMS program. GEMS also gratefully acknowledges the contribution of word processing equipment from Apple Computer, Inc. Under a grant from the National Science Foundation, GEMS Leader's Workshops have been held across the country. For further information on GEMS leadership opportunities, please contact GEMS at the address and phone number below.

©1989 by The Regents of the University of California. All rights reserved. Printed in the United States of America. Reprinted with revisions, 1991.

International Standard Book Number: 0-912511-19-2

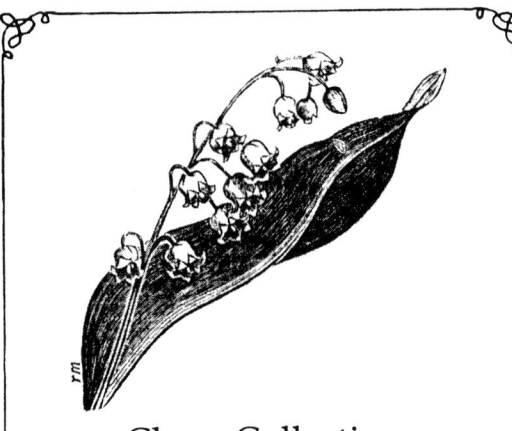

Chase Collection

Center for Environmental Education

Antioch New England Graduate School Library

wood engraving by Randy Miller

## COMMENTS WELCOME

Great Explorations in Math and Science (GEMS) is an ongoing curriculum development project. GEMS guides are revised periodically, to incorporate teacher comments and new approaches. We welcome your criticisms, suggestions, helpful hints, and any anecdotes about your experience presenting GEMS activities. Your suggestions will be reviewed each time a GEMS guide is revised. Please send your comments to: GEMS Revisions, c/o Lawrence Hall of Science, University of California, Berkeley, CA 94720. The phone number is (415) 642-7771.

# Great Explorations in Math and Science (GEMS) Program

The Lawrence Hall of Science (LHS) is a public science center on the University of California at Berkeley campus. LHS offers a full program of activities for the public, including workshops and classes, exhibits, films, lectures, and special events. LHS is also a center for teacher education and curriculum research and development.

Over the years, LHS staff have developed a multitude of activities, assembly programs, classes, and interactive exhibits. These programs have proven to be successful at the Hall and should be useful to schools, other science centers, museums, and community groups. A number of these guided-discovery activities have been published under the Great Explorations in Math and Science (GEMS) title, after an extensive refinement process that includes classroom testing of trial versions, modifications to ensure the use of easy-to-obtain materials, and carefully written and edited step-by-step instructions and background information to allow presentation by teachers without special background in mathematics or science.

**Staff**
Glenn T. Seaborg, Principal Investigator
Jacqueline Barber, Director
Cary Sneider, Curriculum Specialist
Katharine Barrett, John Erickson, Jaine Kopp, Kimi Hosoume, Laura Lowell, Linda Lipner, Carolyn Willard, Staff Development Specialists
Jan M. Goodman, Mathematics Consultant
Cynthia Ashley, Administrative Coordinator
Gabriela Solomon, Distribution Coordinator
Lisa Haderlie Baker, Art Director
Carol Bevilacqua and Lisa Klofkorn, Designers
Lincoln Bergman and Kay Fairwell, Editors

**Contributing Authors**

| | |
|---|---|
| Leigh Agler | Alan Gould |
| Jeremy Ahouse | Cheryll Hawthorne |
| Jacqueline Barber | Sue Jagoda |
| Katharine Barrett | Jefferey Kaufmann |
| Lincoln Bergman | Robert C. Knott |
| Marion E. Buegler | Larry Malone |
| David Buller | Cary I. Sneider |
| Linda De Lucchi | Elizabeth Stage |
| Jean Echols | Jennifer Meux White |

# Reviewers

We would like to thank the following educators who reviewed, tested, or coordinated the reviewing of this series of GEMS materials in manuscript form. Their critical comments and recommendations contributed significantly to these GEMS publications. Their participation does not necessarily imply endorsement of the GEMS program.

## ARIZONA

**Cheri Balkenbush**
Shaw Butte Elementary School, Phoenix

**Debbie Baratko**
Shaw Butte Elementary School, Phoenix

**Flo-Ann Barwick Campbell**
Mountain Sky Junior High School, Phoenix

**Nancy M. Bush**
Desert Foothills Junior High School, Phoenix

**Sandra Jean Caldwell**
Lakeview Elementary School, Phoenix

**George Casner**
Desert Foothills Junior High School, Phoenix

**Richard Clark***
Washington School District, Phoenix

**Don Diller**
Sunnyslope Elementary School, Phoenix

**Carole Dunn**
Lookout Mountain Elementary School, Phoenix

**Joseph Farrier**
Desert Foothills Junior High School, Phoenix

**Robert E. Foster, III**
Royal Palm Junior High School, Phoenix

**Walter C. Hart**
Desert View Elementary School, Phoenix

**E.M. Heward**
Desert Foothills Junior High School, Phoenix

**Stephen H. Kleinz**
Desert Foothills Junior High School, Phoenix

**Karen Lee**
Moon Mountain Elementary School, Phoenix

**Nancy Oliveri**
Royal Palm Junior High School, Phoenix

**Susan Jean Parchert**
Sunnyslope Elementary School, Phoenix

**Brenda Pierce**
Cholla Junior High School, Phoenix

**C.R. Rogers**
Mountain Sky Junior High School, Phoenix

**Phyllis Shapiro**
Sunset Elementary School, Glendale

**David N. Smith**
Maryland Elementary School, Phoenix

**Leonard Smith**
Cholla Junior High School, Phoenix

**Sandra Stanley**
Manzanita Elementary School, Phoenix

**Roberta Vest**
Mountain View Elementary School, Phoenix

## CALIFORNIA

**Richard Adams***
Montera Junior High School, Oakland

**Gerald Bettman**
Dan Mini Elementary School, Vallejo

**Lee Cockrum***
Pennycook Elementary School, Vallejo

**James A. Coley***
Dan Mini Elementary School, Vallejo

**Deloris Parker Doster**
Pennycook Elementary School, Vallejo

**Jane Erni**
Dan Mini Elementary School, Vallejo

**Dawn Fairbanks**
Columbus Intermediate School, Berkeley

**Jose Franco**
Columbus Intermediate School, Berkeley

**Stanley Fukunaga**
Montera Junior High School, Oakland

**Ann Gilbert**
Columbus Intermediate School, Berkeley

**Karen E. Gordon**
Columbus Intermediate School, Berkeley

**Vana Lee James**
Willard Junior High School, Berkeley

**Dayle Kerstad***
Cave Elementary School, Vallejo

**George J. Kodros**
Piedmont High School, Piedmont

**Jackson Lay***
Piedmont High School, Piedmont

**Margaret Lacrampe**
Sleepy Hollow Elementary School, Orinda

**Chiyomi Masuda**
Columbus Intermediate School, Berkeley

**Kathy Nachbaur Mans**
Pennycook Elementary School, Vallejo

**Lin Morehouse***
Sleepy Hollow Elementary School, Orinda

**Barbara Nagel**
Montera Junior High School, Oakland

**Neil Nelson**
Cave Elementary School, Vallejo

**Tina L. Nievelt**
Cave Elementary School, Vallejo

**Jeannie Osuna-MacIsaac**
Columbus Intermediate School, Berkeley

**Geraldine Piglowski**
Cave Elementary School, Vallejo

**Sandra Rhodes**
Pennycook Elementary School, Vallejo

**James Salak**
Cave Elementary School, Vallejo

**Aldean Sharp**
Pennycook Elementary School, Vallejo

**Bonnie Square**
Cave Elementary School, Vallejo

**Judy Suessmeier**
Columbus Intermediate School, Berkeley

**Phoebe A. Tanner**
Columbus Intermediate School, Berkeley

**Marc Tatar**
University of California Gifted Program

**Carolyn Willard***
Columbus Intermediate School

**Robert L. Wood**
Pennycook Elementary School, Vallejo

## ILLINOIS

**Sue Atac**
Thayer J. Hill Junior High School, Naperville

**Miriam Bieritz**
Thayer J. Hill Junior High School, Naperville

**Betty J. Cornell**
Thayer J. Hill Junior High School, Naperville

**Athena Digrindakis**
Thayer J. Hill Junior High School, Naperville

**Alice W. Dube**
Thayer J. Hill Junior High School, Naperville

**Kurt K. Engel**
Waubonsie Valley High School, Aurora

**Anne Hall**
Thayer J. Hill Junior High School, Naperville

**Linda Holdorf**
Thayer J. Hill Junior High School, Naperville

**Mardie Krumlauf**
Thayer J. Hill Junior High School, Naperville

**Lon Lademann**
Thayer J. Hill Junior High School, Naperville

**Mary Lou Lipscomb**
Thayer J. Hill Junior High School, Naperville

**Bernadine Lynch**
Thayer J. Hill Junior High School, Naperville

**Peggy E. McCall**
Thayer J. Hill Junior High School, Naperville

**Anne M. Martin**
Thayer J. Hill Junior High School, Naperville

**Elizabeth R. Martinez**
Thayer J. Hill Junior High School, Naperville

**Thomas G. Martinez**
Waubonsie Valley High School, Aurora

**Judith Mathison**
Thayer J. Hill Junior High School, Naperville

**Joan Maute**
Thayer J. Hill Junior High School, Naperville

**Mark Pennington**
Waubonsie Valley High School, Aurora

**Sher Renken***
Waubonsie Valley High School, Aurora

**Judy Ronaldson**
Thayer J. Hill Junior High School, Naperville

**Michael Terronez**
Waubonsie Valley High School, Aurora

## KENTUCKY

**Judy Allin**
Rangeland Elementary School, Louisville

**Martha Ash**
Johnson Middle School, Louisville

**Pamela Bayr**
Johnson Middle School, Louisville

**Pam Boykin**
Johnson Middle School, Louisville

**April Bond**
Rangeland Elementary School, Louisville

**Sue M. Brown**
Newburg Middle School, Louisville

**Jennifer L. Carson**
Knight Middle School, Louisville

**Lindagarde Dalton**
Robert Frost Middle School, Louisville

**Tom B. Davidson**
Robert Frost Middle School, Louisville

**Mary Anne Davis**
Rangeland Elementary School, Louisville

**John Dyer**
Johnson Middle School, Louisville

**Tracey Ferdinand**
Robert Frost Middle School, Louisville

**Jane L. Finan**
Stuart Middle School, Louisville

**Susan M. Freepartner**
Knight Middle School, Louisville

**Patricia C. Futch**
Stuart Middle School, Louisville

**Nancy L. Hack**
Stuart Middle School, Louisville

**Mildretta Hinkle**
Johnson Middle School, Louisville

**Barbara Hockenbury**
Rangeland Elementary School, Louisville

**Deborah M. Hornback**
Museum of History and Science, Louisville

**Nancy Hottman***
Newburg Middle School, Louisville
**Brenda W. Logan**
Newburg Middle School, Louisville
**Amy S. Lowen***
Museum of History and Science, Louisville
**Peggy Madry**
Johnson Middle School, Louisville
**Jacqueline Mayes**
Knight Middle School, Louisville
**Debbie Ostwalt**
Stuart Middle School, Louisville
**Gil Polston**
Stuart Middle School, Louisville
**Steve Reeves**
Johnson Middle School, Louisville
**Rebecca S. Rhodes**
Robert Frost Middle School, Louisville
**Patricia A. Sauer**
Newburg Middle School, Louisville
**Donna J. Stevenson**
Knight Middle School, Louisville
**Dr. William McLean Sudduth***
Museum of History and Science, Louisville
**Carol Trussell**
Rangeland Elementary School, Louisville
**Janet W. Varon**
Newburg Middle School, Louisville
**Nancy Weber**
Robert Frost Middle School, Louisville

## MICHIGAN

**John D. Baker**
Portage North Middle School, Portage
**Laura Borlik**
Lake Michigan Catholic Elementary School, Benton Harbor
**Sandra A. Burnett**
Centreville Junior High School, Centreville
**Colleen Cole**
Comstock Northeast Middle School, Comstock
**Sharon Christensen***
Delton-Kellogg Middle School, Delton
**Beth Covey**
The Gagie School, Kalamazoo
**Ronald Collins**
F.C. Reed Middle School, Bridgeman
**Gary Denton**
Gull Lake Middle School, Hickory Corners
**Iola Dunsmore**
Lake Center Elementary School, Portage
**Margaret Erich**
St. Monica Elementary School, Portage
**Stirling Fenner**
Gull Lake Middle School, Hickory Corners
**Richard Fodor**
F.C. Reed Middle School, Bridgeman
**Daniel French**
Portage North Middle School, Portage
**Stanley L. Guzy**
Bellevue Middle School, Bellevue
**Dr. Alonzo Hannaford**
The Gagie School, Kalamazoo
**Barbara Hannaford**
The Gagie School, Kalamazoo
**Karen J. Hileski**
Comstock Northeast Middle School, Comstock
**Suzanne Lahti**
Lake Center Elementary School, Portage
**Dr. Phillip T. Larsen***
Western Michigan University, Kalamazoo
**Sandy Lellis**
Bellevue Middle School, Bellevue
**Betty Meyerink**
F.C. Reed Middle School, Bridgeman

**Rhea Fitzgerald Noble**
Buchanan Middle School, Buchanan
**John O'Toole**
St. Monica Elementary School, Kalamazoo
**Joan A. Rybarczyk**
Lake Michigan Catholic Elementary School, Benton Harbor
**Robert Underly**
Buchanan Middle School, Buchanan

## NEW YORK

**Helene Berman**
Webster Magnet Elementary School, New Rochelle
**Robert Broderick**
Trinity Elementary School, New Rochelle
**Frank Capuzelo**
Albert Leonard Junior High School, New Rochelle
**Michael Colasuonno**
Isaac E. Young Junior High School, New Rochelle
**Antoinette DiGuglielmo**
Webster Magnet Elementary School, New Rochelle
**Linda Dixon**
Scarsdale Junior High School, Scarsdale
**Frank Faraone**
Albert Leonard Junior High School, New Rochelle
**Steven Frantz**
Heathcote Elementary School, Scarsdale
**Richard Golden***
Barnard School, New Rochelle
**Seymour Golden**
Albert Leonard Junior High School, New Rochelle
**Lester Hallerman**
Columbus Elementary School, New Rochelle
**Vincent Iacovelli**
Isaac E. Young Junior High School, New Rochelle
**Cindy Klein**
Columbus Elementary School, New Rochelle
**Donna MacCrae**
Webster Magnet Elementary School, New Rochelle
**Robert Nebens**
George M. Davis Elementary School, New Rochelle
**Eileen Paolicelli**
Ward Elementary School, New Rochelle
**Dr. John V. Pozzi***
City School District of New Rochelle, New Rochelle
**John Russo**
Ward Elementary School, New Rochelle
**Bruce Seiden**
Webster Magnet Elementary School, New Rochelle
**David Selleck**
Albert Leonard Junior High School, New Rochelle
**Charles Yochim**
George M. Davis Elementary School, New Rochelle
**Bruce Zeller**
Isaac E. Young Junior High School, New Rochelle

*Trial test coordinators

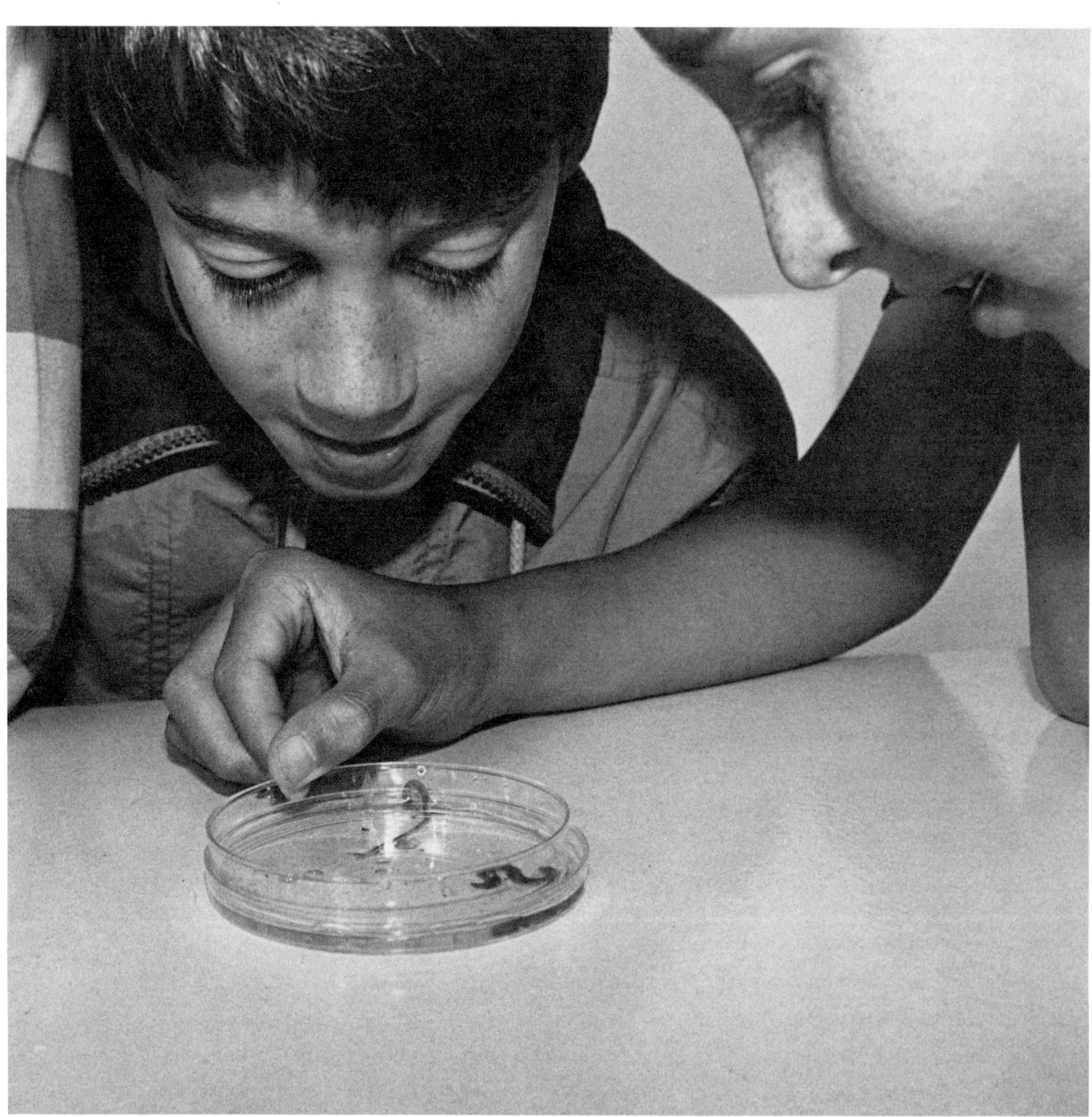

# Contents

Acknowledgments ..................................................... viii

Introduction ................................................................ 1

Session 1: Observing Worms ..................................... 5

Session 2: Worms at Different Temperatures ........... 17

Session 3: Graphing the Data .................................... 25

Going Further ............................................................ 32

Behind the Scenes ...................................................... 34

Resources .................................................................... 39

Summary Outlines ..................................................... 40

Essay on Earthworms ................................................. 42

"Summary Outlines" are provided to help you guide your students through these activities in an organized way. Student data sheets are provided immediately following the session in which they are needed. Additional, removable copies of these data sheets are also included at the back of the booklet.

# Acknowledgments

This activity was initially developed by Robert C. Knott when he taught biology classes in a farming community near Sacramento, California where students wondered "why?" and we all took time to find out what we could about worms and other living things. It has since been presented in biology classes at the Lawrence Hall of Science. Special thanks to Lincoln Bergman for helping the author incorporate the comments and suggestions made by teachers during the GEMS testing process. These teachers are acknowledged at the front of this booklet.

For this second edition we would also like to thank the GEMS enthusiasts who detected errors in the first edition, and GEMS Staff Development Specialist Kimi Hosoume for her help in correcting these errors, and generally revising this edition. The article entitled "Something You Can Do—If You Don't Have Time to Patch the Ozone Hole" is by Doris Gove and is reprinted with permission from the World Journal of the Unitarian Universalist Association in Boston. The essay was called to our attention by Sigrin Thorson Newell, a GEMS Leader who also assisted in the review process for other GEMS publications. "Ode to the Earthworm" was composed by Lincoln Bergman.

# Introduction

Most students are familiar with earthworms, but often only associate them with fishing or rain puddles. In fact, earthworms are very interesting animals in their own right. Their ingestion of old leaves plays a part in the decomposition process, by which nature's nutrients are broken down and returned to the soil. Earthworms also stir up the soil through their eating and thus help aerate the soil.

Earthworms have no eyes, yet can burrow through and obtain food from soil. They can adapt to a wide variety of environmental conditions they may encounter, such as variations in temperature, wetness, and soil compaction.

The activities in this guide provide an enjoyable opportunity for your students to learn about the responses of earthworms to temperature. In Session 1 students have an opportunity to learn more about earthworms through direct observation. Among other things, the students discover that they can see blood coursing through the blood vessel under the skin on the animals' backs. You may want to emphasize this in preparation for the experiments about "pulse" in the next session.

In Session 2, the students experiment to discover the responses of earthworms to three different temperatures. In Session 3, they graph the data gathered during Session 2 and have an opportunity to discuss why earthworms might respond the way they do. During this last session you have an opportunity to help your students understand a little more about "cold-blooded" animals. These activities can be related to a number of curriculum areas, including units on invertebrates, warm and cold-blooded animals, the circulatory system in humans and animals, and ecological and environmental studies.

In the "Behind the Scenes" section on page 32, some background information on earthworms is provided. It should be stressed that the primary goal of these activities is for students to perform the experiments and draw their own conclusions. You may find the background information helpful in answering some student questions, and in guiding the summarizing classroom discussions, but keep the primary goal of direct student experimentation and experience in mind.

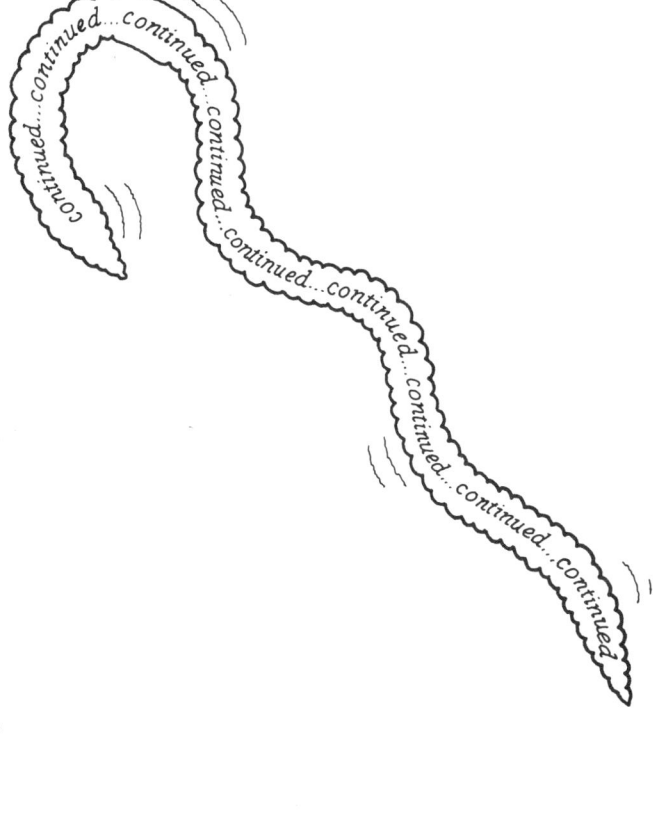

Please pay careful attention to the instructions regarding which sort of earthworm is best for the purposes of this experiment. This information is provided under "Obtaining the Worms" on page 6. Using worms in which the pulse is difficult to see will only prove frustrating to you and your students. Remember that small, pink worms are best. After reading the instructions, you should have no difficulty obtaining an adequate number of appropriate earthworms.

At several points in the text, there are suggestions to the teacher regarding humane care of the earthworms by the students. It is important that students treat their earthworms with care, and recognize that they are living creatures. Some students may need to be reassured that the light pressure on the worms and their placement in water is not harmful to them. As mentioned in the background information, earthworms are capable of obtaining oxygen from the water for short periods of time. Other students may need to be cautioned against applying too much pressure or in any other ways harming the earthworms. Under no circumstances should students experiment at temperatures higher than 35°C. Please read "Maintaining the Worms" on page 32, so you will know how to take good care of them. Once the experiments have been completed, the earthworms should be returned to their natural habitat.

## Ode to the Earthworm

*A pause to thank this worm of earth*
*Through which some of life's nutrients*
*come to birth*
*The butt of many jokes and hurt*
*Tunneler in tons and tons of dirt*
*The leaves that fall from autumn trees*
*Ingested in part by worms like these*
*Mixed in the soil, so new plants thrive*
*Earthworm labor keeps people alive*
*Small pinkish thing of so much worth*
*We thank you gently worm of earth.*

# *Time Frame*

## Session 1: Observing Worms

| | |
|---|---|
| Observing Worms | 5-10 minutes |
| Counting Pulses | 10 minutes |
| Sorting the Earthworms | 7 minutes |
| Cleanup | 8 minutes |
| Discussing the Results | 10 minutes |

## Session 2: Worms at Different Temperatures

| | |
|---|---|
| Experimenting | 40 minutes |
| Cleanup | 5 minutes |

## Session 3: Graphing the Data

| | |
|---|---|
| Review | 10 minutes |
| Graphing the Data | 10 minutes |
| Discussion and Analysis | 25 minutes |

*Please note*: The times listed above are approximations, based on teaching experience in a variety of classroom situations. Having an assistant or parent volunteer in the class during the first two sessions can be very helpful.

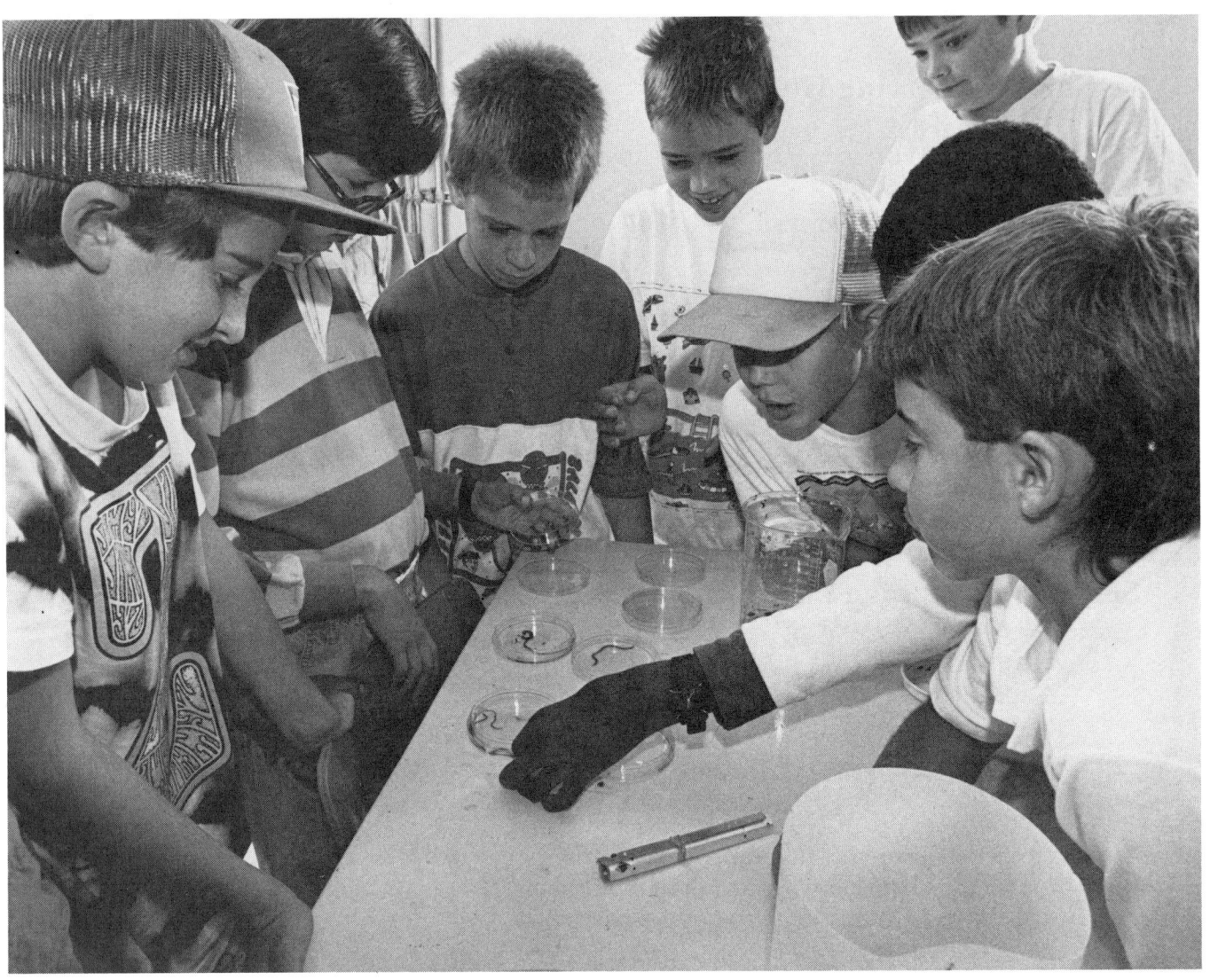

# Session 1: Observing Worms

## Overview

In this session, the students observe earthworms, getting a sense of the earthworms' general activity level. They notice how the worms move, turn themselves over, and how the skin looks and feels. Internal anatomy is also observed. The students will see the blood vessel along the backs of the worms—it is here you will want to focus the students' attention.

Blood pulses through this vessel of the earthworm much like it does in human blood vessels, and the pulses may be counted in a similar manner. For the majority of this session, your students will practice locating and counting earthworm pulses. They will then sort the worms, for use in the following session, selecting those in which the pulse may be most easily seen.

## What You Need

### For the class:

- ☐ 1 timepiece so you or the students can measure 30-second intervals. A classroom clock with a minute hand that "jumps" every minute may also be used.
- ☐ 3 gallons of pond or river water, or aged tap water. (To age water, in order to remove the chlorine, let it sit in an open container for 12 hours.)
- ☐ 1 thermometer for water
- ☐ several water misters

### For each team of two students:

- ☐ 2 moist paper towels
- ☐ 2 earthworms (see "Obtaining the Worms" on the next page)
- ☐ 1 plastic Petri dish (top and bottom)
- ☐ 1 pencil
- ☐ 1 piece of white paper, 8 1/2" X 11"
- ☐ *(optional)* 2 clear plastic cups
- ☐ *(optional)* 1 magnifying lens. May help students see pulse more easily, especially if the lens is large enough to view the entire worm at once. Smaller plastic lenses may make the moving pulse more difficult to see by not magnifying a large enough area.

*High school biology laboratories are usually equipped with Petri dishes, so you may be able to borrow them from that source. They are also available through scientific supply house catalogs.*

# Getting Ready

## One Week Before the Activity:

### Obtaining The Worms:

1. Redworms (*Eisenia foetida*) are the best to use because they are small and light in color. The light, clear skin makes viewing the blood surging through the vessel easier. Larger worms, such as the nightcrawler, are usually not suitable because of their thick and darkly pigmented skin.

2. Worms may be dug up from a garden, field, or compost pile, or purchased from a bait store. Enlist the help of students to bring in earthworms from their yard or garden. A plastic container or bag with some damp soil is ideal for transporting and maintaining the worms.

3. For this experiment you need worms that are 2–4 inches long and visibly pink along the back. The pinkness is caused by the red blood in animals with little or no skin pigment. This activity depends on the students being able to see the pulse in the blood vessel that lies just under the skin on the back of the animal, so it is important to have a selection of "pinkish" worms that will yield at least one suchusable worm for every two students (see the illustration on page 11).

4. Rinse the worms off, in aged water, to make sure you can see the pulse in at least half of the worms needed for your class size. If your worms look pink but you are unable to see the pulsations in a well-lighted room, place the earthworms in some oatmeal for a couple of days, making sure to keep the oatmeal moist. This treatment will help a little because it removes soil from out of the intestine that lies just under the blood vessel.

5. Do the entire activity to help anticipate any problems or questions that may arise. The procedure for observing the earthworm's pulse is described on pages 10 and 11. Also make sure to read "Behind the Scenes" on page 32, for information on maintaining the worms.

6. Decide in advance how you want to conduct the timing procedure. One wrist watch per each team of two students is best. If you decide to have the student teams do their own timing, ask students who have wrist watches to be sure to bring them in for the experiments. If you will be timing for the entire class, you can use the classroom clock or your watch.

**The Day of the Activity:**

1. Assemble the materials. Rinse out the Petri dishes if they are dirty. **DO NOT USE SOAP.**

2. Examine the earthworms to make sure they are alive and well. Healthy earthworms move when touched, and usually move quite a bit when exposed to light or air, or when a water drop hits them. Separate the earthworms from the soil, rinse them in the aged water, and place them in a container of wet paper towels.

3. Set up one or two distribution stations in the classroom from which students can obtain their materials.

4. Make sure that the area where the students will be observing the earthworms is well-lighted. Observing the worms where windows provide daylight, or with good indoor lighting, will be helpful in locating the pulse.

## Observing Worms

*It is also important to gently reinforce ideas about humane treatment of animals with all your students whenever appropriate.*

1. Tell the students you have some earthworms for them to observe today. Ask, "What do you know about earthworms?" "What do they do?" "Where do they live?" While many students are familiar with worms, most have not taken the opportunity to look at them more closely.

2. To address the negative attitudes toward earthworms, present this activity as an opportunity to learn more about an interesting creature that contributes greatly to the recycling of nutrients in the earth. (Pre-selection of teams can also help by pairing squeamish students with others who are less concerned about handling worms during the experiment.)

3. Tell the students that they will be observing the behavior, and the internal and external anatomy, of the earthworms. Assure the class that they will not be dissecting the worms, or harming them in any way. Explain that all of the worms will be returned to the soil after each activity.

4. Form teams of two. Ask one student from each team to get two worms and place them on wet paper towels or in wet clear plastic cups. Mention that because the earthworms are "breathing" the oxygen through their wet skin, the worm must be kept moist at all times. Have a few water misters at the distribution stations for the students to share.

5. Allow at least 10 minutes for observation. Assign a Recorder for each team to take notes. Explain to the students that worms are fragile animals and can be hurt easily, so the students should be gentle with them.

6. Suggest that teams observe their worm by watching and comparing its movements on wet an dry surfaces and its response to water, touch, darkness. Students may gently touch the worm with a damp finger. If the worm is in a plastic cup or on a Petri dish, internal structures can be seen if the worm is viewed from below. Ask, "Which end is the head? the tail? What can you see inside of the earthworm?"

7. Circulate among the teams and assist them in making observations about the earthworm's behavior and structures. Help the students to notice the heart and blood vessel. Encourage them to look for the blood moving along inside that vessel. The pulsing action can also be described as the vessel alternately swelling and contracting. A magnifier or hand lens that is large enough to view the whole worm can be helpful in seeing the pulse.

8. When the students are finished, have the teams return the earthworms to the damp paper towels at the distribution stations. All materials should be rinsed (without soap) and returned to the stations.

9. Bring the class back together and ask each team to be ready to share their observations with the class. Draw a simple outline of a worm on the board, large enough for all to see. Students can come up and draw, label, or make notes on the drawing to record their observations, identifying the blood vessel, the heart, segments, clitellum, anterior and posterior ends, etc.

10. Call attention to any observations of the blood vessel, heart, and movement of blood. Ask students to describe the blood flow. Is there a pattern to the pulsing? Which direction does it flow? What is the blood transporting? [oxygen, waste, nutrients] Use the drawing on the board to illustrate the discussion.

11. After all of the observations have been discussed, introduce the term *adaptation*. Describe adaptation as the characteristics and behaviors of an organism that help it to survive in its environment. Lead a discussion about how the different structures and behaviors of the earthworm might help it to survive in its underground home.

12. Tell the students that they will be investigating the characteristic of blood flow in an earthworm by taking its pulse. Invite the students to suggest how they might take the pulse of an earthworm. [Count the pulses of blood going through that blood vessel in one minute.]

# Counting the Pulses

## Demonstrating How To Count The Pulse

1. Explain to the students that one way to see the pulse involves placing a worm into a little bit of water and covering it with a clear dish. Assure them that putting the worm in water does not harm it. Demonstrate the procedure as follows:

   a. Dip the top of the Petri dish (the larger half of the dish) into the container of aged water, to fill it to about 1/4 inch.

   b. Add one earthworm to the container.

   c. Place it on a white surface so the earthworm can be seen more clearly.

   d. Then nest the bottom (the smaller half of the Petri dish) flat side down inside the larger dish, onto the water and the earthworm, as shown in the diagram. The plastic should be lightly touching the earthworm's back and flattening it just a little. If the plastic does not contact the earthworm easily, students should not press down harder on the plastic, but instead they should discard some of the water by tipping the entire system over a paper towel. If the worm is being pressed too tightly, water should be added.

   e. Look down at the earthworm to see the pulse.

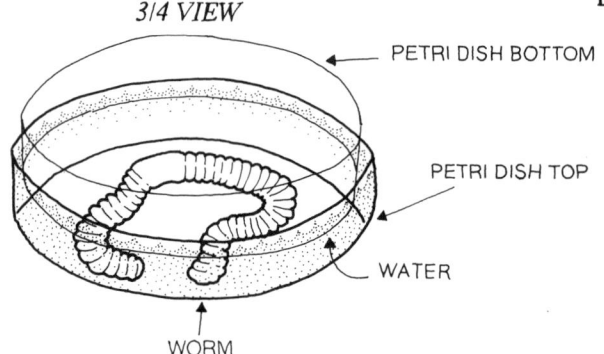

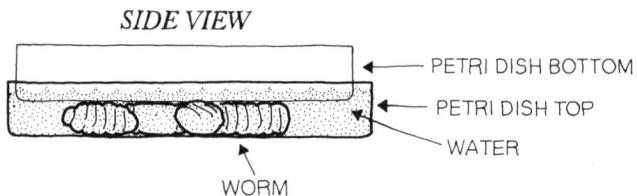

*Several teachers have suggested making a transparency of the worm and its circulatory system. Emphasize to the students that they are looking for something that moves and pulses, so they should not focus on just one small spot.*

2. Invite a few students to locate the blood vessel on the top side (or dorsal side) of your demonstration earthworm and to determine when a pulse occurs. Explain that a pulse is a single enlargement of the dorsal vessel as the blood passes through the vessel from the tail toward the head. Tell the students that there is also a vessel on the underside (or ventral side) of the worm, but it is more difficult to see. Which direction do they think the blood flows in this ventral vessel? [from head to tail]

3. Write the following report form on the chalkboard. The students will copy this form onto a piece of paper and fill in the data as they measure their worm's pulse. Have the students take the temperature of the aged water in the class container and record it.

| WATER TEMP | TRIAL 1 30 SEC. RATE | TRIAL 2 30 SEC. RATE | SUM OF 1 & 2 | DIV. BY 2 | AVE. # PULSES 30 SEC. | TIMES TWO (X2) | AVE PULSE PER MIN. |
|---|---|---|---|---|---|---|---|
| _____ | _____ + | _____ = | _____ | /2 = | _____ | X 2 = | _____ |

4. Explain each step, emphasizing the following:
Trial 1 + Trial 2 / 2 = AVERAGE 30-second pulse.
The AVERAGE 30-second pulse X 2 = the pulse rate per minute.

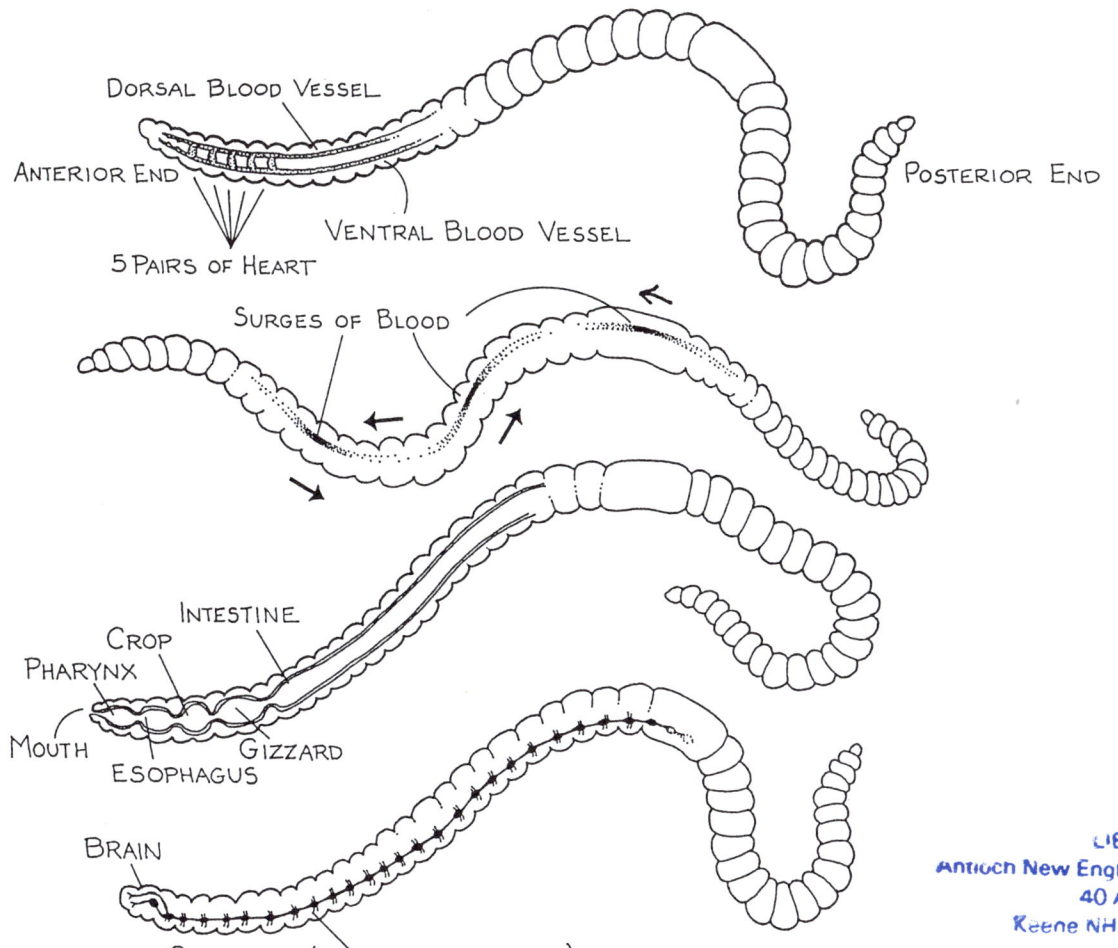

Session 1  11

# Pulse Taking

1. Distribute one blank sheet to each pair of students and ask them to copy the pulse recording form you put on the board. The students, in teams of two, count the pulses in an earthworm for 30 seconds. If you are counting for the students, tell them you will call out "Ready, Ready, Count" as your second hand nears some convenient point. You will then call out "Stop" after 30 seconds. Students will count the pulse twice, record the count on their recording form, and then average the results. If the students are timing themselves, designate one student as the timer and the other as the pulse counter. The students can then switch roles on successive trials, in order to alternate the counting opportunities.

2. Divide the students into teams of two. Let each team obtain one Petri dish (both parts), water from the distribution station(s), an earthworm, and the paper. Have them begin work.

3. Assist the students in locating and counting the pulses. If the students are unable to see the pulse, they may still be able to see a reddening caused by a surge of red blood, a clearing, then another surge, etc.

4. Students having difficulty seeing a pulse for the first time might find it easier if they move to an area with natural light. Removing some slight amount of water may be helpful in preventing the worm from moving too much. Suggest that students having difficulty observe a group that has already located the pulse, to get a better idea of what they should see.

5. Have students obtain another worm if they are having trouble viewing the pulse in their first worm.

*Note*: The earthworm pulse rate at average room temperature of 22°C will probably be between 18 and 26 pulses per minute. Don't tell the students any specific number, but let them know they are not looking for a fast pulse.

6. Have the teams measure and record the two 30-second pulse rates on the white paper. Ask them to average these two separate counts and record the average pulse rate. To average the counts, students should add the two counts and divide by 2.

7. Circulate among the teams to see how they are doing, and assist those having difficulty. If most of the pulse rates are within a range of about 10 pulses, assume the students are probably counting correctly. If the range is much wider, consider having teams do two more trials, switching team roles, or trying a different worm from another team. For younger students, you may also want to consider pairing students who seem to be counting successfully with those who are having more difficulty. Be alert for students who become so caught up by the rhythm of counting that they are not really counting in synchrony with the pulse. Ask students to count quietly so as not to disturb others.

## Sorting the Earthworms

1. Before cleaning up, ask the students to sort your entire supply of earthworms into two groups:

>    a. those with pulses that are easy to see, and

>    b. those with pulses that are not easy to see.

2. Provide two labelled containers, each with moist soil, in which the students can place the worms.

## Clean Up

1. After the students have gathered their data and sorted the worms, they should discard the water and wipe out their Petri dishes with a paper towel.

2. Have students return to their seats for a discussion.

# Discussing the Results

1. Ask each team to present their results to the class. Record the average pulse rates on the chalkboard. You may want to make a graph showing the average pulse rates of all the teams in the class. Invite the students to suggest why the counts are not all the same. Students may suggest that:

> • the water temperatures were not all the same.
>
> • the worms may not all be the same.
>
> • the size of the worms might make the pulse rates greater.
>
> • the worms might have individual differences like humans.
>
> • they might have missed counting some pulses.

2. Ask what environmental factors in the natural environment might cause the earthworm's pulse rate to vary? How would having a slower or faster pulse rate benefit an earthworm?

3. Tell the students that during the next session they will measure the worms' pulse rates at different temperatures. Explain that some of the water will be colder and some warmer. Invite them to predict how the earthworms' pulse rates might respond to changing water temperatures. You may want to have the students write their predictions as hypotheses on their data sheets.

*Session 1*

# Session 2: Worms at Different Temperatures

## Overview

In this session, the students measure the pulse rate of earthworms at three different temperatures and record their results on the data sheet. Without the use of a constant temperature water bath, it may be difficult for teacher and students to maintain temperatures to the exact degree. Obviously, time taken to transfer the water and count the pulse will affect the temperatures. While it is important to strive for accuracy, some variation is unavoidable. So long as the temperatures are relatively close to those suggested, and are in contrast to each other, the experiment should provide useful results.

## What You Need

**For the class:**

- ☐ 1 two-quart (2 liter) container of water at 5° C. (Wide-mouthed, so you can add ice cubes.)
- ☐ 1 two-quart (2 liter) container of water at room temperature (Wide-mouthed is best, so students can dip Petri dishes into the water without having to pour from a large container.)
- ☐ 1 two-quart (2 liter) wide-mouthed container of water at 35° C. If your tap water is not at least 35°C, you will need to heat the water.
  
  *Note*: For the above three water containers, you could use clean plastic bleach containers with their tops one-third cut off, other clear plastic containers, large wide-mouthed mayonnaise jars, or any other containers into which students can dip their Petri dishes.
- ☐ 1 container to hold 20 or more ice cubes
- ☐ 1 (or more) thermos or electric coffee pot to hold or heat water to 35°C.
- ☐ 2 gallons (8 liters) aged tap water
- ☐ 1 timepiece so you can measure one-minute intervals.
- ☐ 3 Celsius thermometers
- ☐ 3 labels, or a felt pen to label water temperatures.

**For each team of two students:**

- ☐ *(optional)* 1 magnifying lens
- ☐ 1 plastic Petri dish (top and bottom)
- ☐ 2 earthworms (sorted for ease of pulse counting in Session 1)
- ☐ 1 paper towel
- ☐ 1 container for waste water
- ☐ 1 Student Data Sheet (master included, page 23)
- ☐ 1 pencil

# Getting Ready

1. Duplicate one Student Data Sheet for each team.

2. Assemble the materials. Remember that you will need aged tap water.

3. Use a thermometer to determine if your hot tap water is 35°C or more. If not, you will need to heat about 3 quarts (3 liters) of water.

4. Prepare the three containers of water. From which the students will obtain the water at varying temperatures they need to put into their Petri dishes.

*Note:* We recommend using the Celsius scale thermometers because that is the international standard for temperature measurement in scientific work. Should only Fahrenheit thermometers be available, the conversion formula is: multiply the Celsius temperature by 1.8 and add 32. Thus:

$$35°C = 95°F \qquad 20°C = 68°F \qquad 5°C = 41°F$$

a. Label three containers with 5°C, 20°C, and 35°C labels.

b. Fill the first two containers with about two liters of aged tap water and add one thermometer to each.

c. Add 15–20 ice cubes to the container with water labelled 5° to make it as cold as possible (about 5°C is as cold as you probably can achieve).

d. Fill the 35°C container with about two liters of water that is about 35°C–40°C (it will cool to about 35°C before you are through mixing).

e. The temperature of the aged water you placed in the container labelled 20°C is probably already close to 20° (room temperature is usually about 22°C). If the water in this container needs to be slightly warmer, add a little of the hottest water to it, until it is 20°C. If it needs to be cooler, add a little of the coldest water.

*Session 2*

5. Set out the materials at the distribution stations. It is easier for the students if you separate the earthworms from the soil, rinse them, and place them in a container of wet paper towels. (These are the earthworms already sorted by the students for easier-to-see pulses.)

6. Be ready to maintain the water temperatures in the three containers.

7. **DO NOT EXCEED THE 35°C MAXIMUM FOR WATER TEMPERATURE BECAUSE THE WORMS MAY DIE.** Earthworms will die at temperatures above 38°C, so do not let the students experiment above 35° C.

## Introducing the Activity

1. Tell your students that in today's activity they will be measuring the pulse rates of earthworms at different temperatures.

2. First, they will cool the earthworms to about 5°C, then measure the pulse at 5°C. Then they will measure the pulse rates at 20°C and 35°C, to determine what happens to the pulse at each temperature.

## Introducing the Procedure

Explain the procedure and demonstrate as needed before having the students begin the experiment.

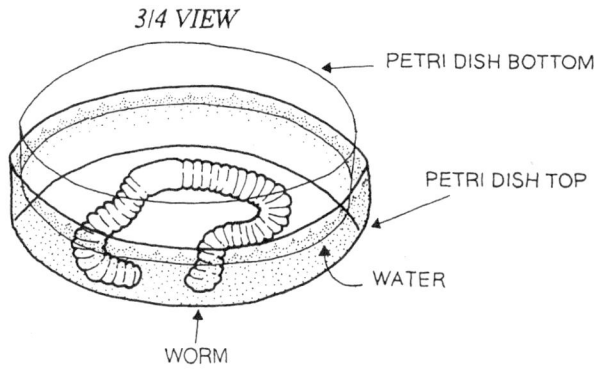

1. Obtain enough 5°C water to fill the top part (the largest part) of a Petri dish one-half full. (The extra water is to help make sure that the worm's temperature starts out as close to 5° as possible.)

2. Place the worm in the Petri dish containing 5°C water for one minute. Observe its behavior.

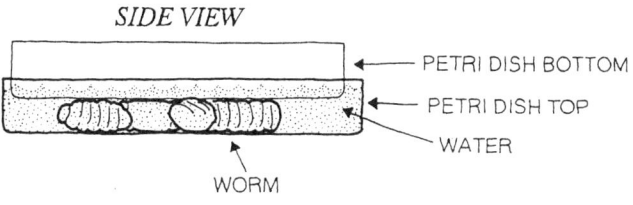

3. Leaving the worm in the dish, pour that water into the waste container. Get more 5°C water, but only 1/4 Petri dish full. Put the top dish on so it presses lightly against the worm's back.

4. Count the pulses and record the number on the data sheet for Trial 1.

5. Count the pulses again and record the number for Trial 2.

6. Average the two pulse rates.

7. Pour the used water into the waste container.

8. Add the next higher temperature water to the same Petri dish, with the same worm in it, and continue as with steps 1-7 above. Fill out the data sheet for Trials 1 and 2 as you proceed and respond to the three questions when the experiments are completed.

## Experimenting

1. Form teams of two. Distribute the data sheets. After the students make their predictions at the top of the Student Data Sheet, let them obtain their materials and begin.

2. Circulate among the students to assist them. If any students are measuring the pulse rates without allowing the worms to become used to each temperature, remind them to wait one minute before taking the pulse.

3. After the students have completed their experiment and recorded their results, collect and save the data sheets for use in the discussion in the next session.

## Clean Up

Ask the students to return the worms to the worm container and to wipe out their Petri dishes. Have them return all materials to the distribution stations, and clean up their work areas.

Names _____

# Student Data Sheet
# Pulse Rates

| TEMPERATURE OF WATER | TRIAL 1 | TRIAL 2 | AVERAGE |
|---|---|---|---|
| 5°C | _____ | _____ | _____ |
| 20°C | _____ | _____ | _____ |
| 35°C | _____ | _____ | _____ |

Describe the behavior of your worms at:

5° _____
_____

20° _____
_____

35° _____
_____

1. What happens to the pulse rate as the worm gets warmer?
_____
_____

2. What happens to the pulse rate as the worm gets colder?
_____
_____

3. At what temperature did your worm seem to be most active?
_____
_____

© 1992 by the Regents of the University of California
LHS–Great Explorations in Math and Science: *Earthworms*

# Session 3: Graphing the Data

## Overview

In this session, your students graph and analyze the results of the previous session's experiment. You then lead the class in a general discussion of possible conclusions that can be drawn from the results and what can be inferred about "cold-blooded" animals such as earthworms.

## What You Need

**For the class:**

❒ chalk

**For each team of two students:**

❒ Student Data Sheets from previous session
❒ Earthworm Graphing Sheets
❒ 1 pencil

1. Using a copy of the Earthworm Graphing Sheet as a guide, sketch a blank graph on the chalkboard for your use during the data collection and discussion.

2. Duplicate one Earthworm Graphing Sheet (page 30) for each team.

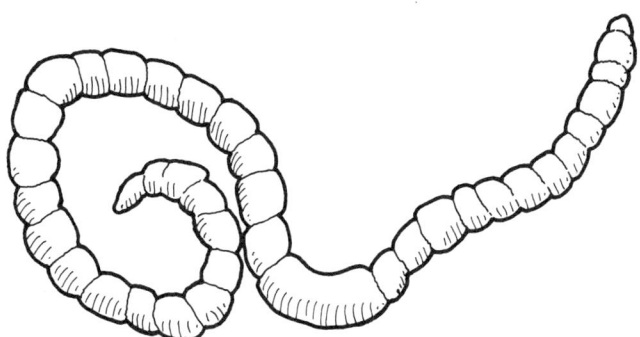

### Graphing the Data

1. Tell the students you will discuss the results of the earthworm pulse rate experiments today, but that before doing this they will need to graph their results.

2. If they are not already familiar with graphing, tell the students that a graph is a way to make a picture of information that is often easier to interpret and understand than the same numbers listed by themselves.

3. Distribute the "Earthworm Graphing Sheet" and explain how they can transfer the data from their data sheets to the graph.

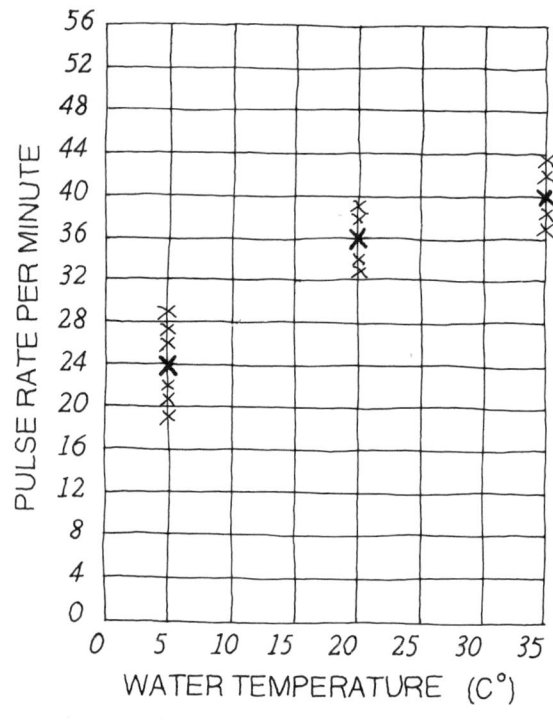

   a. The students should first find the average 1 minute pulse rate for their worm at 5°C, and write that temperature in the first blank on the data sheet.

   b. They should find that number along the bottom of their graph, and follow that line upwards until they reach the horizontal line that is the same as the pulse rate of the worm at that temperature.

   c. They should place a small x at that point.

   d. Repeat this procedure for each of the other two temperature averages.

4. Let the students begin graphing their data.

## Analysis and Discussion

1. After the graphs have been completed, invite the students to give you and the class their results. You might ask questions like: "How many teams had data points that decreased as the temperature went up? How many had data points that increased?"

2. Ask one member from each team to come up and record their three temperature points on your graph.

3. Look at the points recorded for 5° C. Ask, "What is the smallest point recorded? What is the largest?" Explain that by their response, they have just defined the *range.* Help the students identify the *average* number of beats per minute for this range of data points. Use the same procedure to determine the range and average of the pulsebeats recorded by the class for 20° C and for 35° C. The class graph or histogram drawn on the board with these results is very helpful in discussion.

*Some teachers have found it interesting and helpful to summarize the data obtained in a number of classes, also in graph form. For example, if you teach several classes you may want to average all the results. You could make a graph showing all the results, perhaps color-coded by class. This can prompt discussions about whether or not a more accurate average is obtained when there are more results, why there is variation, and what scientists might do when confronted with differing results.*

## Discussing the Results

1. Ask the students to look at the three points that represent the averages of the results at the three temperatures. Ask, "How can we sum up this data?" "Did the heartbeat rates increase or decrease with a rise in temperature?" "Was there more of an increase between 5° C and 20° C, or between 20° C and 35° C? If there is a difference between these two, what might have caused it?

2. Have each team summarize the *behavior* of their earthworms at the three different temperatures. How did the behavior of the worms relate to their heartbeat rates?

3. Ask the students what they think might have caused the earthworm pulses to change when the temperature changed? Typical answers might include:

- That's the way worms are!

- It's like hibernation.

- The blood is thicker and doesn't flow as fast when it's cold.

- The earth is harder to dig (eat) through so the animal may not get as much food and his pulse slows down when he's hungry.

- All growth slows in cold temperatures.

4. Ask the students what explanations they can think of for why it might help an earthworm to survive if its pulse rises when it is warm, and slows down when it is cold? Take a number of responses and lead a discussion. (The "Behind the Scenes" section on page 32 includes additional information.)

5. Remind the students that earthworms are often called "cold-blooded," as are lizards, snakes, and fish. Encourage the students to comment on this name for these animals. You may want to explain to the students that the common term can be somewhat misleading because in actuality the temperature of a "cold-blooded" animal is always the same as its environment. If that environment is cold, then the internal temperature of a "cold-blooded" animal will be cold. However, a lizard on a 39°C rock is probably about 39° C inside its body, if it has been there a long time.

7. Encourage the students to discuss the differences between "warm-blooded" and "cold-blooded" animals. Humans and other "warm-blooded" animals are able to maintain their own body temperatures, regardless of the environment. The discussion will help lead toward an understanding that warm-blooded animals must have a heat-producing and regulating system, while cold-blooded animals do not. Humans are in danger if their temperatures rise from the normal 37.5°C (98.6°F) to 40°C (104°F). So warm-blooded animals must regulate their body temperatures within a narrow range. Warm-blooded animals have the advantage of not having to slow down when their environment is cool, while cold-blooded animals must do so.

8. Ask the students if they have any other ideas or questions about what you've discussed or about earthworms in general. You could discuss their responses to questions 3 and 4 on the graphing sheet. What might happen to the heartbeat rates of earthworms in soil as the soil starts to freeze? Students could experiment further by bringing the water temperatures down to nearly freezing (0° C) in a freezer. Did anyone think of further experiments that might help the class find out more? Write down questions and ideas for possible future discussion and investigation.

Names of Team Members _____

# Earthworm Graphing Sheet

## Earthworm Response To Temperature

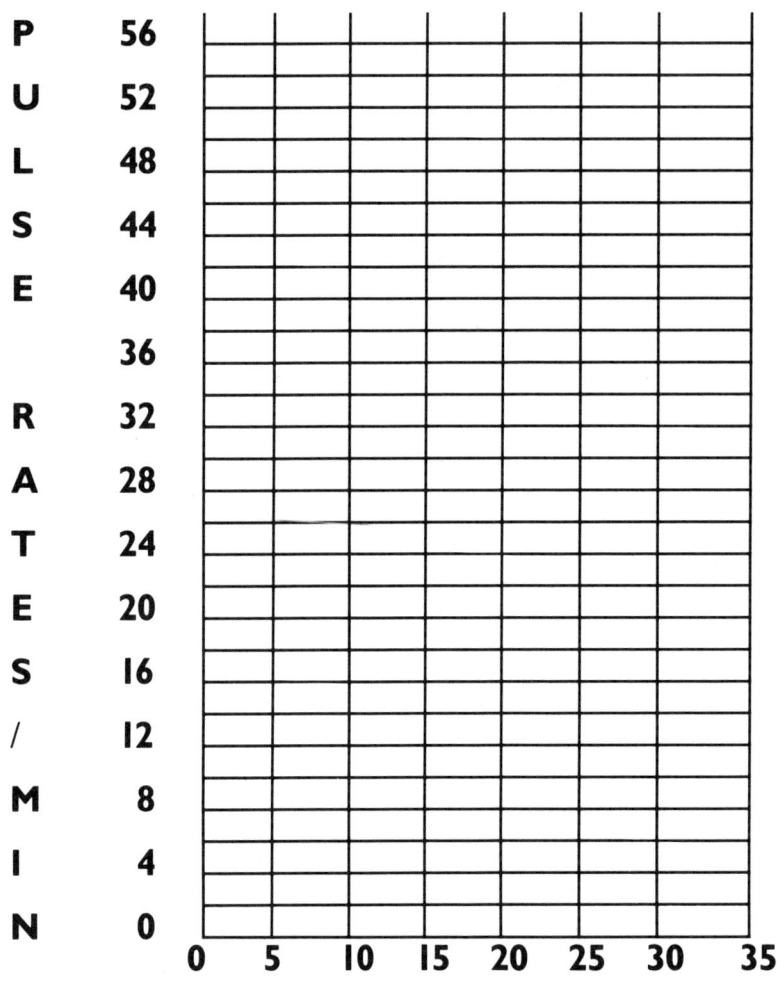

1. Plot the data from the data sheet on to this graph.
2. Based on your graph, what would you expect the pulse rate of an earthworm from a yard to be if the average soil temperature in that yard is 23°C _____
3. Use the graph line to predict what pulse rate you would expect from your earthworm if the water temperature was 30°C _____
4. What pulse rate would you expect if your worm was in 0°C water? _____

30  *Going Further*  © 1992 by the Regents of the University of California
LHS–Great Explorations in Math and Science: *Earthworms*

# Going Further

1. One group of students (Group A) can keep five earthworms at a certain temperature unknown to another group of students (Group B). The B group measures the pulse rates of these five worms and predicts the temperature at which Group A kept the worms before giving the worms to Group B.

2. Measure the average pulse rate of five earthworms that have been in moist soil with humus (food), at room temperature. Maintain these same worms in moist paper towels in a covered container for two days (no food) at the same temperature. Measure their pulse rate again to see if being without food changes their pulse rates. Be sure to keep the paper towels moist at all times.

3. Investigate worm movement related to temperature:

> a. Add about 3" of garden soil to a long tray.
>
> b. Place a light bulb over one end of the tray or a heating pad beneath one end to create the "warm" soil. Place an ice pack under the other end to create the "cool" end.
>
> c. Add some worms to the soil. Make a map showing where you placed the worms.
>
> d. See where the worms are after 24 hours. Measure the temperature at the area of the tray where you find the most worms.

4. Students can lay down layers of several different colors or types of soil in a clear container, moisten the soil, and add three or four large earthworms. Cover the containers with a "sleeve" made of dark construction paper. After only a few days, observe how the layers of soil have been mixed.

## Some Literary Extensions

Have your students imagine what the world would be like to an earthworm. They could write a story that begins with some of their actual observations of earthworm behavior, then extends to their own ideas about how they would view the soil and plants, animals and people, if they were earthworms. The stories could span the four seasons, with descriptions of earthworm behavior in response to rain, snow, heat, floods, and other environmental factors.

If your students want to take off from their study of real-life earthworms into a strange and humorous expedition looking for highly intelligent, gigantic "earthworms" of extraterrestrial origin who communicate by singing and also play chess, they may want to read the book entitled *The Worms of Kukumlima* by Daniel Pinkwater, E.P. Dutton, New York, 1981.

# Behind the Scenes

The information in this section is primarily for your reference. It is not meant to be read out loud to or distributed to your students before they have done the activities.

## Maintaining The Worms

**Container:** Worms may be kept in any clean, waterproof container. A smooth, high-sided container, such as a clear plastic water or bleach bottle, prevents the worms from escaping. If such a container is no more than 2/3 full of soil, it allows plenty of air for the worms, even if the container is covered for up to 24 hours.

**Medium:** The best solution is to keep the worms in the same medium (usually soil) they were in when you found them. Garden soil or peat moss works well. Potting soil is not recommended. Be certain to keep the worms out of direct sunlight.

**Moisture:** Note the dampness of the soil or other medium and maintain that level. Do not allow the soil to become dry!

**Temperature:** Any temperature between 40°F (4°C) and 90°F (32°C) is fine.

**Air:** Earthworms do not need much air, but if you cover the container of worms with a solid lid, be sure to uncover it for an hour or so every 24 hours. Perforating the lid is helpful, but even this lid must be removed for an hour or so every two days.

## General Background

Earthworms have five aortic arches ("hearts") in the blood vessel that pump blood from the front end to the back end along the underside of the worm and back to the hearts along the top of the worm. Blood movement along the upper vessel can be seen by the unaided eye.

Worms eat vegetable matter that is ground up in a gizzard and which then passes through the digestive cavity.

Worms have no lungs or special breathing parts. Oxygen and carbon dioxide are respectively absorbed and exhausted through the skin. That is why, if water has enough oxygen in it, worms can be immersed in it for limited periods of time and survive.

Earthworms are "cold-blooded" animals, but this common term is something of a misnomer. Like other "cold-blooded" animals, their blood is not really cold unless their environment is cold. The worms simply have no regulating mechanism or the ability to make heat, so they are the same temperature as the environment. The temperature of a worm's environment determines the activity level of the animal. The scientific term for this is *poikilothermic.*

Earthworm pulse rates rise as the temperature rises. As noted in the text, earthworms die at temperatures above 38°C, so, to be on the safe side, do not let the students experiment at temperatures above 35° C. Earthworms are made of protein and protein breaks down (denatures) at about 40°C. That's why an egg white, also protein, will fry (break down and turn white) on a 40°C. sidewalk, if left long enough.

# Adaptability and Survival

As is the case with all living things, both plant and animal, earthworms have characteristics that enable them to live in certain defined niches. These niches include specific combinations and ranges of environmental factors such as light, temperature, moisture, pressure. If the environmental factors go beyond the acceptable range a particular organism can stand, it will die unless it can move to a new area.

The earthworm lives inside small-diameter tubes inside the earth. The earth must be moist or the worm, with its porous skin, would lose all of its moisture to the dry soil. The worm literally eats through the soil to make the tubes and tunnels, so moist soil also means easier tunneling, which in turn means more food per minute, a healthier worm, increased reproduction, and thus more worms. A richer food supply can promote these changes too.

Many other environmental factors can also influence worm response and behavior. As this activity indicates, the response of earthworms to temperature indicates a high degree of adaptability and helps them survive. For example, in situations where temperature change is somewhat gradual or seasonal, the worm can burrow to a more hospitable level (downward in a midwestern winter, upward in the summer).

If the temperature drops too low, the worm's metabolism also drops greatly, even to the point where the worm may not move or eat. If a worm is trapped in this cold, such as when its passage is blocked by a rock or water-soaked base in the soil, a cold worm, with significantly lowered metabolism, can often survive without food because it isn't digesting anything or using much energy. If the worm can keep its energy use very low, it can survive for more than a month, by which time the earth may warm up and conditions improve.

When too much water enters a worm tunnel, problems can also arise. Tunnels can become blocked with debris, or plug up completely. The worm loses some of the friction necessary to crawl/wiggle forward, and its gas exchange (oxygen in, carbon dioxide out) is restricted. The worm responds to high concentrations of water in the tunnel by trying to avoid it and escape. Escaping to a more habitable tunnel, or to a protected location above ground, allows the worm to survive and reproduce, thus helping preserve the species.

Such adaptability is wonderful, and it helps explain why, after millions of years, the species is so plentiful and so ubiquitous.

*Your students may wonder why, if water in tunnels presents dangers to earthworms, they can be safely placed in the Petri dishes with water in them and still "breathe." In the small tube filled with water, the water interferes with the worm's respiration by limiting the surface area available for the exchange of gases to take place, while in the dish there is sufficient surface area available for the worm to obtain oxygen from the water itself for a limited period of time.*

# Resources

In addition to the World Book or other encyclopedias and biology reference books you may have available, the following are useful references. There are many other excellent books and articles on earthworms.

Applehof, Mary: *Worms Eat My Garbage: How to set up and maintain a worm composting system.* Flower Press, Kalamazoo, Michigan, 1982.

Campbell, Stu: *Let It Rot, The Gardener's Guide to Composting*, Storey Publishing, Pownal, Vermont, revised edition 1990.

*Elementary Science Study, Teacher's Guide for Earthworms.* Delta Education, Nashua, New Hampshire, 1971.

Hess, Lilo: *The Amazing Earthworm.* Scribner's, New York, 1979.

Kramer, David C: "Earthworms. (The Classroom Animal)." *Science and Children*, March 1986, pages 33—34.

McLaughlin, Molly: *Earthworms, Dirt, and Rotten Leaves*, Atheneum, MacMillan Publishing Company, New York, 1986.

McDonald, Charlotte J: "Do Worms Have Feelings?" and McGuire, Daniel C: "Project Worm Bin," in *Science and Children*, March 1987, pages 8—13. This issue of the National Science Teacher's Association (NSTA) magazine also contains other short articles and resource lists on earthworms and related topics.

# Summary Outlines

## Session 1: Observing Worms

**One Week Before the Activity**
1. Obtain earthworms.
2. Evaluate earthworms for pulse visibility.
3. Store earthworms.
4. Ask students to bring wrist watches.
5. Age tap water if you have no pond water.

**The Day of the Activity**
1. Separate earthworms from soil.
2. Sort earthworms.
3. Establish distribution stations.
4. Copy the record form on the board.

**Observing Earthworms**
1. Student observation of worms on wet towels.
2. Gather observations.
3. Demonstrate how to count pulse.
4. Students practice counting.
5. Students sort earthworms.
6. Lead discussion.

## Session 2: Worms at Different Temperatures

**Before the Day of the Activity**
　　Duplicate Student Data Sheet.

**The Day of the Activity**
　　1. Heat water.
　　2. Get ice cubes.
　　3. Prepare water at 3 temperatures.
　　4. Set up distribution stations.

**Taking Pulses at Different Temperatures**
　　1. Demonstrate procedures.
　　2. Students experiment and record.
　　3. Collect Student Data Sheets.

## Session 3: Graphing the Data

**Before the Day of the Activity**
　　Duplicate the graphing sheet.

**The Day of the Activity**
　　Rough copy the graphing sheet onto the board.

**Graphing the Data**
　　1. Distribute the Data Sheets from Session 2.
　　2. Explain graphing procedure.
　　3. Students graph their data.
　　4. Students make a graph on the board with the class data.

**Analysis and Discussion**
　　1. Collect general information.
　　2. Interpret the data by using the graph.
　　3. Hold discussion.
　　　　a. Effect of temperature on pulse rate.
　　　　b. Warm-blooded vs. cold-blooded animals.

*The following essay by Doris Gove, reprinted with permission of the World Journal of the Unitarian Universalist Association, was the first prize winner in an essay contest on the theme: "Respect for the interdependent web of all existence of which we are a part."*

# Something You Can Do If You Don't Have Time to Patch the Ozone Hole

You've seen them—on the sidewalk, pink, stretched out, straight as dandelion stems, hurrying in the wrong direction. From under your umbrella, you've seen them on the street, ground to bits by tires or shoes, pasty-white, the blood washed out of them. Later in the day you've seen them curled, dried to a dark red crisp by the same sun that lifts your spirits after the rain.

Next time it rains hard after a dry spell, rescue worms. Earthworms need airborne oxygen; when their burrows get flooded, they have to come out. Under normal circumstances, the water runs off or soaks deep into the ground, and the worms go home after reveling in the rainy air. They may cross rocks and logs; there's always good earthworm real estate on the other side. How could they know about asphalt strips hundreds of wormlengths wide and thousands of miles long? These exposed, pink, hustling worms are truly needy. Help them.

What's in it for us? Well, shade, for one, and dogwood flowers next spring (they bring in revenue if your city has a dogwood festival), and oxygen for aerobics classes. You remember from high-school—earthworms are decomposers; without them, fields and forests would be in the same solid waste pickle as many cities. You say that stuff about decomposers was boring? Well, let's use a word for the '90s. Recycle. Trees cannot recycle their leaves any more than you can eat Christmas catalogs. The worms do it. They reach out their pointy prehensile snouts and pull leaves into their burrows, coat them with slimy saliva, and process them. And, unlike some folks, they don't want it all. They absorb some nutrients and deposit the rest as euphemized castings, rounded heaps of digested humus. Ready to mainline into trees, grass, or broccoli.

So here you are, standing in the rain, late for work, gazing down at an earthworm crossing your path. The rain slows to a drizzle and light flows through the thinning clouds. The worm before you is at the curb, still straining and purposeful, even though dead wrong. It reaches over the edge, tapping like a white cane. You notice its bright red dorsal blood vessel, zigzagging slightly near the head, but running all the way to the tail. Worms, you remember, have a closed circulatory system, more like ours than their fellow invertebrates, the insects, whose watery blood sloshes around like bilge water.

Here's how to proceed:

**1** Check for traffic.

**2** Tap the worm gently two or three times near the clitellum, that swollen light part that wraps around five or six segments near the head end like a turtleneck scarf. This will make it writhe and become short and fat, easier to pick up.

**3** Pick it up. Or, if you prefer, coax it onto a leaf or your Visa card.

**4** Place it on a good nearby burrow building site, which is probably where it came from anyway. Make sure it is three-to-four feet back from the pavement so it won't wander out again.

**5** Wipe your hands on your clothes.

**6** (Optional) If people stare, either; a) invite them to help; or b) talk to the worm as you pick it up.

Once you have done this, you are involved. You can't pick up just one. Now surely, you argue when you reach the sobering environment of your office, there are plenty of worms in the soil, and it won't matter if some get fried, especially considering that efficient mating system they have.

Perhaps true. But they are as alive as any stranded whale or harp seal pup.

And if you do get into the worm habit, evangelize. Invite a co-worker to contribute a rainy day coffee break. Patrol sidewalks with the kids. Make your neighborhood safe for wormkind. Take your child's class on a worm rescue mission and talk about humans and original recycling.

And the next time you present your Visa card at a fine department store, explain why it feels a bit sticky. ●

# MORE ON THEMES

The word "themes" is used in many different ways in both ordinary usage and in educational circles. In the GEMS series, themes are seen as key recurring ideas that cut across all the scientific disciplines. Themes are bigger than facts, concepts, or theories. They link various theories from many disciplines. They have also been described as "the sap that runs through the curriculum," to convey the sense that they permeate through and arise from the curriculum. By listing the themes that run through a particular GEMS unit on the title page, we hope to assist you in seeing where the unit fits into the "big picture" of science, and how the unit connects to other GEMS units. The theme "Patterns of Change," for example, suggests that the unit or some important part of it exemplifies larger scientific ideas about why, how, and in what ways change takes place, whether it be a chemical reaction or a caterpillar becoming a butterfly. GEMS has selected 10 major themes:

**Systems & Interactions**  **Scale**
**Models & Simulations**  **Structure**
**Stability**  **Energy**
**Patterns of Change**  **Matter**
**Evolution**  **Diversity & Unity**

If you are interested in thinking more about themes and the thematic approach to teaching and constructing curriculum, you may wish to obtain a copy of our handbook, *To Build A House: GEMS and the Thematic Approach to Teaching Science*. For more information and an order brochure, write or call GEMS, Lawrence Hall of Science, University of California, Berkeley, CA 94720. (415) 642-7771. **Thanks for your interest in GEMS!**

## TEACHER'S GUIDES

Acid Rain
  Grades 6–10
Animal Defenses
  Preschool–K
Animals in Action
  Grades 5–9
Bubble-ology
  Grades 5–9
Buzzing a Hive
  Preschool–3
Chemical Reactions
  Grades 6–10
Color Analyzers
  Grades 5–8
Convection: A Current Event
  Grades 6–9
Crime Lab Chemistry
  Grades 4–8
Discovering Density
  Grades 6–10
Earth, Moon & Stars
  Grades 5–9
Earthworms
  Grades 6–10
Experimenting with Model Rockets
  Grades 6–10
Fingerprinting
  Grades 4–8
Global Warming
  Grades 7–10
Height-O-Meters
  Grades 6–10
Hide a Butterfly
  Preschool–3
Hot Water & Warm Homes from Sunlight
  Grades 4–8
Involving Dissolving
  Grades 1–3
Liquid Explorations
  Grades K–3
Mapping Animal Movements
  Grades 5–9
Mapping Fish Habitats
  Grades 6–10
More Than Magnifiers
  Grades 6–9
Of Cabbages & Chemistry
  Grades 4–8
Oobleck: What Do Scientists Do?
  Grades 4–8
Paper Towel Testing
  Grades 5–8
QUADICE
  Grades 4–8
River Cutters
  Grades 6–9
Vitamin C Testing
  Grades 4–8

## ASSEMBLY PRESENTER'S GUIDES

The "Magic" of Electricity
  Grades 3–6
Solids, Liquids, and Gases
  Grades 3–6

## EXHIBIT GUIDES

Shapes, Loops & Images
  all ages
The Wizard's Lab
  all ages

## SUPPLEMENTARY MATERIALS

GEMS Teacher's Handbook
GEMS Leader's Handbook
A Parent's Guide to GEMS
To Build a House: GEMS &
  the Thematic Approach to
  Teaching Science

● *Please contact the GEMS project for a descriptive brochure and ordering information.*

*Write or call*
GEMS
Lawrence Hall of Science
University of California at Berkeley  94720
(510) 642-7771

Names _____

# Student Data Sheet
# Pulse Rates

| TEMPERATURE OF WATER | TRIAL 1 | TRIAL 2 | AVERAGE |
|---|---|---|---|
| 5°C | _____ | _____ | _____ |
| 20°C | _____ | _____ | _____ |
| 35°C | _____ | _____ | _____ |

Describe the behavior of your worms at:

5° _____
_____

20° _____
_____

35° _____
_____

1. What happens to the pulse rate as the worm gets warmer?
_____
_____

2. What happens to the pulse rate as the worm gets colder?
_____
_____

3. At what temperature did your worm seem to be most active?
_____
_____

Names of Team Members _____

# Earthworm Graphing Sheet

## Earthworm Response To Temperature

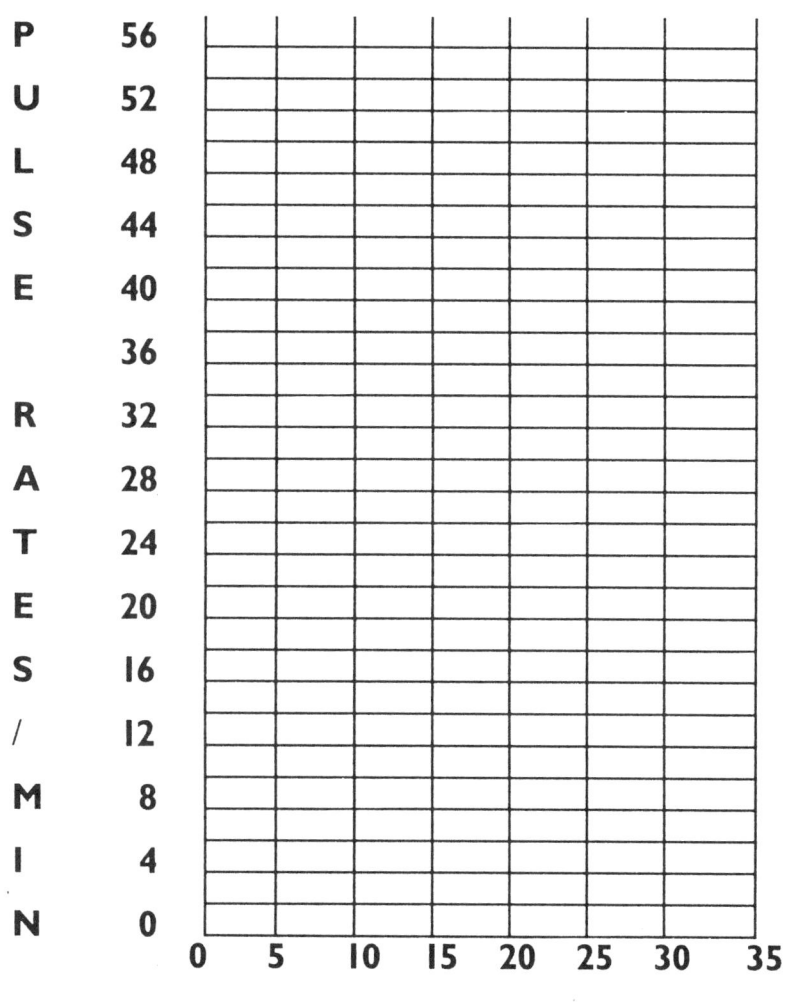

**WATER TEMPERATURE [°C]**

1. Plot the data from the data sheet on to this graph.
2. Based on your graph, what would you expect the pulse rate of an earthworm from a yard to be if the average soil temperature in that yard is 23°C _____
3. Use the graph line to predict what pulse rate you would expect from your earthworm if the water temperature was 30°C _____
4. What pulse rate would you expect if your worm was in 0°C water? _____

© 1992 by the Regents of the University of California
LHS–Great Explorations in Math and Science: *Earthworms*

*Notes*